SCRIPTURE
JOURNAL

ENGLISH STANDARD VERSION

1–2 PETER
&
JUDE

CROSSWAY

WHEATON, ILLINOIS — ESV.ORG

ESV® Scripture Journal: 1–2 Peter and Jude

The Holy Bible, English Standard Version® (ESV®)
Copyright © 2001 by Crossway,
a publishing ministry of Good News Publishers.
All rights reserved.

ESV® Text Edition: 2016

Printed in China
Published by Crossway
Wheaton, Illinois 60187, U.S.A.
crossway.org

Crossway is a not-for-profit publishing ministry that exists solely for the purpose of publishing the Good News of the Gospel and the Truth of God's Word, the Bible. A portion of the purchase price of every ESV Bible is donated to help support Bible distribution ministry around the world.

The ESV Bible is free online and on mobile devices everywhere worldwide, including a selection of free Bible resources, at esv.org.

RRDS	26	25	24	23	22	21	20	19	18	17
12	11	10	9	8	7	6	5	4	3	2	1

PREFACE

The Bible

The words of the Bible are the very words of God our Creator speaking to us. They are completely truthful;[1] they are pure;[2] they are powerful;[3] and they are wise and righteous.[4] We should read these words with reverence and awe,[5] and with joy and delight.[6] Through these words God gives us eternal life,[7] and daily nourishes our spiritual lives.[8]

The ESV Translation

The English Standard Version® (ESV®) stands in the classic stream of English Bible translations that goes back nearly five centuries. In this stream, accurate faithfulness to the original text is combined with simplicity, beauty, and dignity of expression. Our goal has been to carry forward this legacy for this generation and generations to come.

The ESV is an "essentially literal" translation that seeks as far as possible to reproduce the meaning and structure of the original text and the personal style of each Bible writer. We have sought to be "as literal as possible" while maintaining clear expression and literary excellence. Therefore the ESV is well suited for both personal reading and church ministry, for devotional reflection and serious study, and for Scripture memorization.

---

[1] Ps. 119:160; Prov. 30:5; Titus 1:2; Heb. 6:18 [2] Ps. 12:6 [3] Jer. 23:29; Heb. 4:12; 1 Pet. 1:23
[4] Ps. 19:7–11 [5] Deut. 28:58; Ps. 119:74; Isa. 66:2 [6] Ps. 19:7–11; 119:14, 97, 103; Jer. 15:16
[7] John 6:68; 1 Pet. 1:23 [8] Deut. 32:46; Matt. 4:4

The ESV Publishing Team

The ESV publishing team has included more than a hundred people. The fourteen-member Translation Oversight Committee benefited from the work of fifty biblical experts serving as Translation Review Scholars and from the comments of the more than fifty members of the Advisory Council. This international team from many denominations shares a common commitment to the truth of God's Word and to historic Christian orthodoxy.

To God's Honor and Praise

We know that no Bible translation is perfect; but we also know that God uses imperfect and inadequate things to his honor and praise. So to God the Father, Son, and Holy Spirit—and to his people—we offer what we have done, with our prayers that it may prove useful, with gratitude for much help given, and with ongoing wonder that our God should ever have entrusted to us so momentous a task.

To God alone be the glory!
The Translation Oversight Committee

1 PETER

Greeting

1 Peter, an apostle of Jesus Christ,
To those who are elect exiles of the Dispersion in Pontus, Galatia, Cappadocia, Asia, and Bithynia, [2] according to the foreknowledge of God the Father, in the sanctification of the Spirit, for obedience to Jesus Christ and for sprinkling with his blood:
May grace and peace be multiplied to you.

Born Again to a Living Hope

[3] Blessed be the God and Father of our Lord Jesus Christ! According to his great mercy, he has caused us to be born again to a living hope through the resurrection of Jesus Christ from the dead, [4] to an inheritance that is imperishable, undefiled, and unfading, kept in heaven for you, [5] who by God's power are being guarded through faith for a salvation ready to be revealed in the last time. [6] In this you rejoice, though now for a little while, if necessary, you have been grieved by various trials, [7] so that the tested genuineness of your faith—more precious than gold that perishes though it is tested by fire—may be found to result in praise and glory and honor at the revelation of Jesus Christ. [8] Though you have not seen him, you love him. Though you do not now see him, you believe in him and rejoice with

joy that is inexpressible and filled with glory, [9] obtaining the outcome of your faith, the salvation of your souls.

[10] Concerning this salvation, the prophets who prophesied about the grace that was to be yours searched and inquired carefully, [11] inquiring what person or time the Spirit of Christ in them was indicating when he predicted the sufferings of Christ and the subsequent glories. [12] It was revealed to them that they were serving not themselves but you, in the things that have now been announced to you through those who preached the good news to you by the Holy Spirit sent from heaven, things into which angels long to look.

Called to Be Holy

[13] Therefore, preparing your minds for action, and being sober-minded, set your hope fully on the grace that will be brought to you at the revelation of Jesus Christ. [14] As obedient children, do not be conformed to the passions of your former ignorance, [15] but as he who called you is holy, you also be holy in all your conduct, [16] since it is written, "You shall be holy, for I am holy." [17] And if you call on him as Father who judges impartially according to each one's deeds, conduct yourselves with fear throughout the time of your exile, [18] knowing that you were ransomed from the futile ways inherited from your forefathers, not with perishable things such as silver or gold, [19] but with the precious blood of Christ, like that of a lamb without blemish or spot. [20] He was foreknown before the foundation of the world but was made manifest in the last times for the sake of you [21] who through him are believers in God, who raised him from the dead and gave him glory, so that your faith and hope are in God.

²²Having purified your souls by your obedience to the truth for a sincere brotherly love, love one another earnestly from a pure heart, ²³since you have been born again, not of perishable seed but of imperishable, through the living and abiding word of God; ²⁴for

"All flesh is like grass
     and all its glory like the flower of grass.
  The grass withers,
     and the flower falls,
²⁵   but the word of the Lord remains forever."

And this word is the good news that was preached to you.

A Living Stone and a Holy People

2 So put away all malice and all deceit and hypocrisy and envy and all slander. ²Like newborn infants, long for the pure spiritual milk, that by it you may grow up into salvation— ³if indeed you have tasted that the Lord is good.

⁴As you come to him, a living stone rejected by men but in the sight of God chosen and precious, ⁵you yourselves like living stones are being built up as a spiritual house, to be a holy priesthood, to offer spiritual sacrifices acceptable to God through Jesus Christ. ⁶For it stands in Scripture:

"Behold, I am laying in Zion a stone,
     a cornerstone chosen and precious,
  and whoever believes in him will not be put to
     shame."

[7] So the honor is for you who believe, but for those who do not believe,

> "The stone that the builders rejected
>   has become the cornerstone,"

[8] and

> "A stone of stumbling,
>   and a rock of offense."

They stumble because they disobey the word, as they were destined to do. [9] But you are a chosen race, a royal priesthood, a holy nation, a people for his own possession, that you may proclaim the excellencies of him who called you out of darkness into his marvelous light. [10] Once you were not a people, but now you are God's people; once you had not received mercy, but now you have received mercy.

[11] Beloved, I urge you as sojourners and exiles to abstain from the passions of the flesh, which wage war against your soul. [12] Keep your conduct among the Gentiles honorable, so that when they speak against you as evildoers, they may see your good deeds and glorify God on the day of visitation.

Submission to Authority

[13] Be subject for the Lord's sake to every human institution, whether it be to the emperor as supreme, [14] or to governors as sent by him to punish those who do evil and to praise those who do good. [15] For this is the will of God, that by doing good

you should put to silence the ignorance of foolish people. ¹⁶ Live as people who are free, not using your freedom as a cover-up for evil, but living as servants of God. ¹⁷ Honor everyone. Love the brotherhood. Fear God. Honor the emperor.

¹⁸ Servants, be subject to your masters with all respect, not only to the good and gentle but also to the unjust. ¹⁹ For this is a gracious thing, when, mindful of God, one endures sorrows while suffering unjustly. ²⁰ For what credit is it if, when you sin and are beaten for it, you endure? But if when you do good and suffer for it you endure, this is a gracious thing in the sight of God. ²¹ For to this you have been called, because Christ also suffered for you, leaving you an example, so that you might follow in his steps. ²² He committed no sin, neither was deceit found in his mouth. ²³ When he was reviled, he did not revile in return; when he suffered, he did not threaten, but continued entrusting himself to him who judges justly. ²⁴ He himself bore our sins in his body on the tree, that we might die to sin and live to righteousness. By his wounds you have been healed. ²⁵ For you were straying like sheep, but have now returned to the Shepherd and Overseer of your souls.

Wives and Husbands

3 Likewise, wives, be subject to your own husbands, so that even if some do not obey the word, they may be won without a word by the conduct of their wives, ² when they see your respectful and pure conduct. ³ Do not let your adorning be external—the braiding of hair and the putting on of gold jewelry, or the clothing you wear— ⁴ but let your adorning be the hidden person of the heart with the imperishable beauty of a gentle and quiet spirit, which in God's sight is very

precious. [5] For this is how the holy women who hoped in God used to adorn themselves, by submitting to their own husbands, [6] as Sarah obeyed Abraham, calling him lord. And you are her children, if you do good and do not fear anything that is frightening.

[7] Likewise, husbands, live with your wives in an understanding way, showing honor to the woman as the weaker vessel, since they are heirs with you of the grace of life, so that your prayers may not be hindered.

Suffering for Righteousness' Sake

[8] Finally, all of you, have unity of mind, sympathy, brotherly love, a tender heart, and a humble mind. [9] Do not repay evil for evil or reviling for reviling, but on the contrary, bless, for to this you were called, that you may obtain a blessing. [10] For

"Whoever desires to love life
and see good days,
let him keep his tongue from evil
and his lips from speaking deceit;
[11]   let him turn away from evil and do good;
let him seek peace and pursue it.
[12]   For the eyes of the Lord are on the righteous,
and his ears are open to their prayer.
But the face of the Lord is against those who
do evil."

[13] Now who is there to harm you if you are zealous for what is good? [14] But even if you should suffer for righteousness' sake, you will be blessed. Have no fear of them, nor be troubled,

¹⁵ but in your hearts honor Christ the Lord as holy, always being prepared to make a defense to anyone who asks you for a reason for the hope that is in you; yet do it with gentleness and respect, ¹⁶ having a good conscience, so that, when you are slandered, those who revile your good behavior in Christ may be put to shame. ¹⁷ For it is better to suffer for doing good, if that should be God's will, than for doing evil.

¹⁸ For Christ also suffered once for sins, the righteous for the unrighteous, that he might bring us to God, being put to death in the flesh but made alive in the spirit, ¹⁹ in which he went and proclaimed to the spirits in prison, ²⁰ because they formerly did not obey, when God's patience waited in the days of Noah, while the ark was being prepared, in which a few, that is, eight persons, were brought safely through water. ²¹ Baptism, which corresponds to this, now saves you, not as a removal of dirt from the body but as an appeal to God for a good conscience, through the resurrection of Jesus Christ, ²² who has gone into heaven and is at the right hand of God, with angels, authorities, and powers having been subjected to him.

Stewards of God's Grace

4 Since therefore Christ suffered in the flesh, arm yourselves with the same way of thinking, for whoever has suffered in the flesh has ceased from sin, ² so as to live for the rest of the time in the flesh no longer for human passions but for the will of God. ³ For the time that is past suffices for doing what the Gentiles want to do, living in sensuality, passions, drunkenness, orgies, drinking parties, and lawless idolatry. ⁴ With respect to this they are surprised when you do not join

them in the same flood of debauchery, and they malign you; ⁵ but they will give account to him who is ready to judge the living and the dead. ⁶ For this is why the gospel was preached even to those who are dead, that though judged in the flesh the way people are, they might live in the spirit the way God does.

⁷ The end of all things is at hand; therefore be self-controlled and sober-minded for the sake of your prayers. ⁸ Above all, keep loving one another earnestly, since love covers a multitude of sins. ⁹ Show hospitality to one another without grumbling. ¹⁰ As each has received a gift, use it to serve one another, as good stewards of God's varied grace: ¹¹ whoever speaks, as one who speaks oracles of God; whoever serves, as one who serves by the strength that God supplies—in order that in everything God may be glorified through Jesus Christ. To him belong glory and dominion forever and ever. Amen.

Suffering as a Christian

¹² Beloved, do not be surprised at the fiery trial when it comes upon you to test you, as though something strange were happening to you. ¹³ But rejoice insofar as you share Christ's sufferings, that you may also rejoice and be glad when his glory is revealed. ¹⁴ If you are insulted for the name of Christ, you are blessed, because the Spirit of glory and of God rests upon you. ¹⁵ But let none of you suffer as a murderer or a thief or an evildoer or as a meddler. ¹⁶ Yet if anyone suffers as a Christian, let him not be ashamed, but let him glorify God in that name. ¹⁷ For it is time for judgment to begin at the household of God; and if it begins with us, what will be the outcome for those who do not obey the gospel of God? ¹⁸ And

> "If the righteous is scarcely saved,
>> what will become of the ungodly and the
>>> sinner?"

[19] Therefore let those who suffer according to God's will entrust their souls to a faithful Creator while doing good.

Shepherd the Flock of God

5 So I exhort the elders among you, as a fellow elder and a witness of the sufferings of Christ, as well as a partaker in the glory that is going to be revealed: [2] shepherd the flock of God that is among you, exercising oversight, not under compulsion, but willingly, as God would have you; not for shameful gain, but eagerly; [3] not domineering over those in your charge, but being examples to the flock. [4] And when the chief Shepherd appears, you will receive the unfading crown of glory. [5] Likewise, you who are younger, be subject to the elders. Clothe yourselves, all of you, with humility toward one another, for "God opposes the proud but gives grace to the humble."

[6] Humble yourselves, therefore, under the mighty hand of God so that at the proper time he may exalt you, [7] casting all your anxieties on him, because he cares for you. [8] Be sober-minded; be watchful. Your adversary the devil prowls around like a roaring lion, seeking someone to devour. [9] Resist him, firm in your faith, knowing that the same kinds of suffering are being experienced by your brotherhood throughout the world. [10] And after you have suffered a little while, the God of all grace, who has called you to his eternal glory in Christ, will himself restore, confirm, strengthen, and establish you. [11] To him be the dominion forever and ever. Amen.

Final Greetings

¹²By Silvanus, a faithful brother as I regard him, I have written briefly to you, exhorting and declaring that this is the true grace of God. Stand firm in it. ¹³She who is at Babylon, who is likewise chosen, sends you greetings, and so does Mark, my son. ¹⁴Greet one another with the kiss of love.

Peace to all of you who are in Christ.

2 PETER

Greeting

1 Simeon Peter, a servant and apostle of Jesus Christ,
To those who have obtained a faith of equal standing with
ours by the righteousness of our God and Savior Jesus Christ:

² May grace and peace be multiplied to you in the knowledge of God and of Jesus our Lord.

Confirm Your Calling and Election

³ His divine power has granted to us all things that per-
tain to life and godliness, through the knowledge of him
who called us to his own glory and excellence, ⁴ by which he
has granted to us his precious and very great promises, so
that through them you may become partakers of the divine
nature, having escaped from the corruption that is in the
world because of sinful desire. ⁵ For this very reason, make
every effort to supplement your faith with virtue, and virtue with knowledge, ⁶ and knowledge with self-control, and
self-control with steadfastness, and steadfastness with godliness, ⁷ and godliness with brotherly affection, and brotherly
affection with love. ⁸ For if these qualities are yours and are
increasing, they keep you from being ineffective or unfruit-
ful in the knowledge of our Lord Jesus Christ. ⁹ For whoever lacks these qualities is so nearsighted that he is blind,

having forgotten that he was cleansed from his former sins.
¹⁰ Therefore, brothers, be all the more diligent to confirm
your calling and election, for if you practice these qualities
you will never fall. ¹¹ For in this way there will be richly pro-
vided for you an entrance into the eternal kingdom of our
Lord and Savior Jesus Christ.

¹² Therefore I intend always to remind you of these qualities, though you know them and are established in the truth
that you have. ¹³ I think it right, as long as I am in this body,
to stir you up by way of reminder, ¹⁴ since I know that the putting off of my body will be soon, as our Lord Jesus Christ made
clear to me. ¹⁵ And I will make every effort so that after my
departure you may be able at any time to recall these things.

Christ's Glory and the Prophetic Word

¹⁶ For we did not follow cleverly devised myths when we
made known to you the power and coming of our Lord Jesus
Christ, but we were eyewitnesses of his majesty. ¹⁷ For when he
received honor and glory from God the Father, and the voice
was borne to him by the Majestic Glory, "This is my beloved
Son, with whom I am well pleased," ¹⁸ we ourselves heard
this very voice borne from heaven, for we were with him on
the holy mountain. ¹⁹ And we have the prophetic word more
fully confirmed, to which you will do well to pay attention
as to a lamp shining in a dark place, until the day dawns and
the morning star rises in your hearts, ²⁰ knowing this first of
all, that no prophecy of Scripture comes from someone's own
interpretation. ²¹ For no prophecy was ever produced by the
will of man, but men spoke from God as they were carried
along by the Holy Spirit.

False Prophets and Teachers

2 But false prophets also arose among the people, just as there will be false teachers among you, who will secretly bring in destructive heresies, even denying the Master who bought them, bringing upon themselves swift destruction. [2] And many will follow their sensuality, and because of them the way of truth will be blasphemed. [3] And in their greed they will exploit you with false words. Their condemnation from long ago is not idle, and their destruction is not asleep.

[4] For if God did not spare angels when they sinned, but cast them into hell and committed them to chains of gloomy darkness to be kept until the judgment; [5] if he did not spare the ancient world, but preserved Noah, a herald of righteousness, with seven others, when he brought a flood upon the world of the ungodly; [6] if by turning the cities of Sodom and Gomorrah to ashes he condemned them to extinction, making them an example of what is going to happen to the ungodly; [7] and if he rescued righteous Lot, greatly distressed by the sensual conduct of the wicked [8] (for as that righteous man lived among them day after day, he was tormenting his righteous soul over their lawless deeds that he saw and heard); [9] then the Lord knows how to rescue the godly from trials, and to keep the unrighteous under punishment until the day of judgment, [10] and especially those who indulge in the lust of defiling passion and despise authority.

Bold and willful, they do not tremble as they blaspheme the glorious ones, [11] whereas angels, though greater in might and power, do not pronounce a blasphemous judgment against them before the Lord. [12] But these, like irrational animals, creatures of instinct, born to be caught and destroyed, blaspheming about matters of which they are ignorant, will also be destroyed

in their destruction, [13] suffering wrong as the wage for their wrongdoing. They count it pleasure to revel in the daytime. They are blots and blemishes, reveling in their deceptions, while they feast with you. [14] They have eyes full of adultery, insatiable for sin. They entice unsteady souls. They have hearts trained in greed. Accursed children! [15] Forsaking the right way, they have gone astray. They have followed the way of Balaam, the son of Beor, who loved gain from wrongdoing, [16] but was rebuked for his own transgression; a speechless donkey spoke with human voice and restrained the prophet's madness.

[17] These are waterless springs and mists driven by a storm. For them the gloom of utter darkness has been reserved. [18] For, speaking loud boasts of folly, they entice by sensual passions of the flesh those who are barely escaping from those who live in error. [19] They promise them freedom, but they themselves are slaves of corruption. For whatever overcomes a person, to that he is enslaved. [20] For if, after they have escaped the defilements of the world through the knowledge of our Lord and Savior Jesus Christ, they are again entangled in them and overcome, the last state has become worse for them than the first. [21] For it would have been better for them never to have known the way of righteousness than after knowing it to turn back from the holy commandment delivered to them. [22] What the true proverb says has happened to them: "The dog returns to its own vomit, and the sow, after washing herself, returns to wallow in the mire."

The Day of the Lord Will Come

3 This is now the second letter that I am writing to you, beloved. In both of them I am stirring up your sincere mind by way of reminder, [2] that you should remember the

predictions of the holy prophets and the commandment of the Lord and Savior through your apostles, ³ knowing this first of all, that scoffers will come in the last days with scoffing, following their own sinful desires. ⁴ They will say, "Where is the promise of his coming? For ever since the fathers fell asleep, all things are continuing as they were from the beginning of creation." ⁵ For they deliberately overlook this fact, that the heavens existed long ago, and the earth was formed out of water and through water by the word of God, ⁶ and that by means of these the world that then existed was deluged with water and perished. ⁷ But by the same word the heavens and earth that now exist are stored up for fire, being kept until the day of judgment and destruction of the ungodly.

⁸ But do not overlook this one fact, beloved, that with the Lord one day is as a thousand years, and a thousand years as one day. ⁹ The Lord is not slow to fulfill his promise as some count slowness, but is patient toward you, not wishing that any should perish, but that all should reach repentance. ¹⁰ But the day of the Lord will come like a thief, and then the heavens will pass away with a roar, and the heavenly bodies will be burned up and dissolved, and the earth and the works that are done on it will be exposed.

¹¹ Since all these things are thus to be dissolved, what sort of people ought you to be in lives of holiness and godliness, ¹² waiting for and hastening the coming of the day of God, because of which the heavens will be set on fire and dissolved, and the heavenly bodies will melt as they burn! ¹³ But according to his promise we are waiting for new heavens and a new earth in which righteousness dwells.

Final Words

¹⁴ Therefore, beloved, since you are waiting for these, be diligent to be found by him without spot or blemish, and at peace. ¹⁵ And count the patience of our Lord as salvation, just as our beloved brother Paul also wrote to you according to the wisdom given him, ¹⁶ as he does in all his letters when he speaks in them of these matters. There are some things in them that are hard to understand, which the ignorant and unstable twist to their own destruction, as they do the other Scriptures. ¹⁷ You therefore, beloved, knowing this beforehand, take care that you are not carried away with the error of lawless people and lose your own stability. ¹⁸ But grow in the grace and knowledge of our Lord and Savior Jesus Christ. To him be the glory both now and to the day of eternity. Amen.

JUDE

Greeting

¹ Jude, a servant of Jesus Christ and brother of James,

To those who are called, beloved in God the Father and kept for Jesus Christ:

² May mercy, peace, and love be multiplied to you.

Judgment on False Teachers

³ Beloved, although I was very eager to write to you about our common salvation, I found it necessary to write appealing to you to contend for the faith that was once for all delivered to the saints. ⁴ For certain people have crept in unnoticed who long ago were designated for this condemnation, ungodly people, who pervert the grace of our God into sensuality and deny our only Master and Lord, Jesus Christ.

⁵ Now I want to remind you, although you once fully knew it, that Jesus, who saved a people out of the land of Egypt, afterward destroyed those who did not believe. ⁶ And the angels who did not stay within their own position of authority, but left their proper dwelling, he has kept in eternal chains under gloomy darkness until the judgment of the great day— ⁷ just as Sodom and Gomorrah and the surrounding cities, which likewise indulged in sexual immorality and pursued unnatural desire, serve as an example by undergoing a punishment of eternal fire.

⁸ Yet in like manner these people also, relying on their dreams, defile the flesh, reject authority, and blaspheme the glorious ones. ⁹ But when the archangel Michael, contending with the devil, was disputing about the body of Moses, he did not presume to pronounce a blasphemous judgment, but said, "The Lord rebuke you." ¹⁰ But these people blaspheme all that they do not understand, and they are destroyed by all that they, like unreasoning animals, understand instinctively. ¹¹ Woe to them! For they walked in the way of Cain and abandoned themselves for the sake of gain to Balaam's error and perished in Korah's rebellion. ¹² These are hidden reefs at your love feasts, as they feast with you without fear, shepherds feeding themselves; waterless clouds, swept along by winds; fruitless trees in late autumn, twice dead, uprooted; ¹³ wild waves of the sea, casting up the foam of their own shame; wandering stars, for whom the gloom of utter darkness has been reserved forever.

¹⁴ It was also about these that Enoch, the seventh from Adam, prophesied, saying, "Behold, the Lord comes with ten thousands of his holy ones, ¹⁵ to execute judgment on all and to convict all the ungodly of all their deeds of ungodliness that they have committed in such an ungodly way, and of all the harsh things that ungodly sinners have spoken against him." ¹⁶ These are grumblers, malcontents, following their own sinful desires; they are loud-mouthed boasters, showing favoritism to gain advantage.

A Call to Persevere

¹⁷ But you must remember, beloved, the predictions of the apostles of our Lord Jesus Christ. ¹⁸ They said to you, "In the last time there will be scoffers, following their own ungodly

passions." [19] It is these who cause divisions, worldly people, devoid of the Spirit. [20] But you, beloved, building yourselves up in your most holy faith and praying in the Holy Spirit, [21] keep yourselves in the love of God, waiting for the mercy of our Lord Jesus Christ that leads to eternal life. [22] And have mercy on those who doubt; [23] save others by snatching them out of the fire; to others show mercy with fear, hating even the garment stained by the flesh.

Doxology

[24] Now to him who is able to keep you from stumbling and to present you blameless before the presence of his glory with great joy, [25] to the only God, our Savior, through Jesus Christ our Lord, be glory, majesty, dominion, and authority, before all time and now and forever. Amen.